THE DAUGHTER

SOUMYA SINGH

Dedicated to Lord Shiva and the love of a mother and a daughter

Contents

Preface *vii*

Acknowledgements *xi*

Prologue *xiii*

1. Unanswered Question 1
2. Mother : Bound By Traditions, Torn By Needs 3
3. Main Business : Dealing With Domestic Violence 6
   Side Business : Journey Of Being The School Supreme
4. The Sweet Admirer 9
5. The Heart Crush 12
6. Sab Mithyaa Hai 15
7. The Ultimate Training Of Being A Homemaker 18
8. What Have I Done Wrong? 23
9. Welcome To The World Of Toxic Growth 27
10. Freedom Or No Freedom? 31
11. How Does It Feel To Take Stand For One's Own Self? How Do We Do It? 35
12. Keeping Them Enriched 39
13. All Energy Drained, Nothing More To Offer 42
14. It's Now Father's Turn 47
15. It Feels Like A Newborn. She Wants To Start All Over Again! 50
16. She Does Not Want To Fight Anymore. It Kills Her. 55

Contents

17. Ripped And Wrecked, More Than Ever 58

18. Those Cold Memories Haunt Her 61

19. The Great Repentance : Break Then Make Initiative 65

20. Welcome To The " Third Generation" 69

21. Kill Her Or Heal Her 72

22. Women Empowerment : It's Time We Do It Right! 76

23. This Time The Daughter Wants To Be A Complete Failure! 80

24. You Cannot Have Best Of Both The Worlds. Never! 84

Preface

This book is the daughter's attempt to make his father understand the real meaning of "women empowerment". It is her sincerest urge that the father really accepts the meaning of "women empowerment" in the truest sense. She feels that it is now high time that he understands it and lets the ladies of the house live their respective lives on their own terms. Just because he has the power of initiating domestic violence anytime and everytime in the house to establish fear in the minds of the housemates, it does not mean that he can impose his definition of women empowerment on the daughter as well. She strongly believes that every person has their own weaknesses and strengths which eventually let them blossom into a unique and a beautiful kind of human being, a human being who must be appreciated and accepted as they are. After all, the mother, the daughter and her younger sibling are also accepting the father as he is! So, he must also learn to accept them as they are and grant them the required freedom to be themselves. It is their priorities and beliefs which will form them and help them achieve what they want. Therefore, instead of controlling their minds and making them fearful through his perfect weapon of "domestic violence", he must give them their share of freedom and when time will be right, they will automatically become "empowered".

Butchering of people's wishes, dreams, thinking to suit his own needs is very selfish and must be stopped by the father. Moreover, labeling all this with a decent name of "empowerment" is pathetic. This is what he has done with the mother and plans the same to do with the daughter. But the daughter denies this. She would like to fight this battle for once before giving up in front of the father because at the end of the day, she does not want to be a loser in her own eyes. She has always known that what has been done with her mother is wrong but she had no choice but to be a mere spectator. Now, when she has grown up and it is her chance to be butchered by the father in the name of "women empowerment", she wants to fight back. She wants to retaliate for her rights.

After living a life of submission for the last 25 years so that peace can prevail in the house, her mind has now gone numb with all the domestic violence that has happened in the house for empowering the mother. She cannot take all this anymore. She wants to start afresh with a father who accepts that what he has done is "sheer butchering" and not "empowerment". She feels that only and only god has the power to dictate us and control our fates, no other human being. Parents must guide us, protect us and but never butcher us to fulfill their own insecurities. An insecurity which the father has been long carrying with the mother because she has outsmarted her in every way must not be made up by bullying the daughter!!! Two people enter into an alliance through marriage, one person outsmarts the other and the other one takes out this frustration on his own daughter by butchering her to be want he wants him to be: a submissive lady who can take care of every bit of the house in the absence of the mother. Wow! What an achievement at the father's end. Two ladies in the house, paying their dues to the father for being how they are supposed to be. Bravo! (Pun intended). The mother paying her dues to the father by bringing money to the house because the father has allowed her to work and be empowered. The daughter paying her dues because she chooses to be on the mother's side and saves her in every single fight from the father. Wow! What a family. And what kind of women empowerment has the father granted to the mother and what kind of empowerment has she achieved where she faces violence for even speaking her own mind?

There is fear, anger and resentment in the heart and mind of the daughter who has been watching this dirty game of the father for the last 25 years. She does not want to let this happen to her, because in the last 25 years, she has understood one thing very clear. This one thing is that the foundation of all this domestic violence is misinterpreted, maligned and distorted definition of "women empowerment" which the father preaches and the mother follows!!! Why does she follow? Why does she not end it once and for all? Is she afraid? No, because now she enjoys it!!! With the daughter being the submissive one towards the father with minimal financial demands (except related to her studies), the mother has found her happiness in her independence which she enjoys through shopping, eating and social gatherings. There is nobody to stop her. The father gives her all these bits of freedom to let her earn more and more money for the house and the daughter does not interrupt in her freedom because she knows that she does not have anything else to keep going !!! The daughter feels that the mother has totally compromised on her principles of dignity and now lives the life which suits the corporate world. Good, good for her. In fact, very good, at least she is able to find solace in this dirty game of the father. But the daughter cannot, because she does not love money at all. She loves true love, a love which frees you from the bondages of "gender inequality" and not the one who makes you enter into yet another bondage of "butchered women empowerment" wherein one person is the master and other has no choice but to be a puppet. Sad pathetic dominance must come to an end. Mentors are there but do not try to be one until you yourself do not know the concepts right. That's why, the daughter, who has always followed the father blindly because she somewhere chose him to be her mentor, does not want to follow him anymore. She first wants him to get his concepts right regarding "women empowerment" and then she can willingly surrender herself to him. But before this, she must fight.

Acknowledgements

I am sincerely thankful to the almighty for giving me the strength and the courage to write this book.

Prologue

Read it if you would like to experience the meaning of true empowerment. Read it for the sake of mankind where everybody wants to flourish on the basis of their unique talents. Read it if you would like to have a look that how an ideal empowered system should work with males and females at the same page, at the same pace leading to a beautifully balanced growth. A sustainble growth as one may say wherein everyone loves to be a part of the process!!!

CHAPTER ONE

Unanswered question

"Go to sleep. You need to get up by 6". These words have been put into daughter's ears by her so called father from the time she has existed on this planet.

Till the time she was in school, these words seemed nice as it helped her to become a better person. Now that she has grown up, these words prick her in the mind as thorns!!

Words remain the same. Meaning has changed. Earlier they were used to make her a better version of herself. At least this is what she thought. Now, as she can see the selfish intentions wrapped around these words, it kills her. The intentions are: "Hey girl, go to sleep, for you have to replace your mother so that she can go to work". Bravo! Earn a living.

"Mother should conquer the outside world. Daughter should conquer the house. After all, it's all about women empowerment. But don't you worry, daughter, you will also get the same kind of platform to grow. Till then, act as a perfect replacement to your mother for household needs." These is the message of the so called father who chooses to act as a victim of private sector unemployment for more than half of his life.

Mother works, grows professionally, sets a good example of a successful women in the society. Now its daughter's turn to do the same. Daughter is well qualified, very much capable to meet the professional expectations of the market. In many ways, it can be said that the daughter is much more capable than the mother to take up all the responsibilities. But there is something which stops her to replace her mother professionally. In this era, where every women wants to change the game and emerge as a leader, what is it that is stopping her??

CHAPTER TWO

Mother : bound by traditions, torn by needs

Father's unemployment issues lead to domestic violence. In the initial years of their marriage, mother chooses to pack her things and go to her brother's house along with her daughter as an act of rebel. She wants to put this message into father's mind that this kind of behavior will not be tolerated.

What happens next???? Well......nothing much! Little drama over the phone with father and then comeback. Comeback of the mother along with her daughter into the same old house. This story repeats for a couple of times. One thing was common when every time she went with her daughter. That single thing was daughter's statement just before the mother used to leave her brother's house to come back. Mother, have you gone mad!! Why are you going back? : this was the statement daughter repeated every time they left for their home.

Time passed. This interesting game of coming and leaving became less frequent and eventually, it stopped. Daughter also realized that this dandi march was of no use as father is a pro at this game and mother is so fearfully bounded by the traditions that the march was merely a march. Nothing more, nothing less. She understood that the march was not meant to create a revolution.

Gradually, daughter and her mother came into terms with the fact that this is how their life is going to be. The most important lesson which they learnt from these upheavals is: It is their own messed up life. It is their own mess. They need to deal with it all alone!!" They realized that the best they could do to deal with this situation is to support each other. Embrace and hold each other tightly, so tightly and stubbornly that father can no longer break them. This is how healing will break through whenever father's demonic ways will be beyond toleration limit. All this awakening came at a cost of few tours to maternal uncle's house but it finally seeped into the minds and hearts of daughter-mother duo. In fact, this time it was deeply embedded into their souls, especially the mother as she accepted that there is no escaping. Daughter was still too young to carry the burden of this acceptance, at least this is what the daughter-mother duo believed. Moreover, when mother completely accepted this harsh truth of life, there was nothing much to be done by the daughter at such an early stage. All she had to do was to obey her mother like a very, very good child. This would give her mother the strength to grow. In return, mother would take care of her needs. And, yes, of course, of the father's three time meals. No one was allowed to forget that!!! It's the most important of all. After all, torn by needs!

A new life began. Laws were laid down. Awakening had come. The saying "Life is governed by simple laws" was realized in full measure. Mother started to grow professionally as her daughter had to be supported.

Daughter was still in school, her education had to be financially supported. Moreover, her whole future was in front of her and money was needed to get the best of the things for her, so that she can grow into a better human being.

Two small families existed within a bigger family!! One family comprised of daughter-mother duo, other family comprised of father. Mother had to take care of both. Although father had always been a minimalistic in his needs (as he never demanded luxury goods for himself) but he focused on quality for his daily essentials and quality comes with a price. Money was spent, mother had to take care of that otherwise violence would be the only way out for the couple. Daughter was her priority in the other world, which was well taken care of.

CHAPTER THREE

Main business : dealing with domestic violence Side business : journey of being the school supreme

The day comprised primarily of father's morning aggressive shoutings waiting eagerly to turn into true domestic violence (thankfully, it mostly never did, mornings were calmer than the evenings, pun intended), going to school, coming back, afternoon sleep and evening domestic violence. Mostly, these evening domestic violence episodes would extend and eventually consume the night as well. It would be around 10 PM till the actual fight used to end. Father would go into another room, preferably the drawing room and daughter- mother duo would sleep in the bedroom. As the father would not be completely satisfied in proving his point, he would come again around 1 or 2 PM into the other room, wake up the sleeping mother, quarrel again and then go back once he has said everything he wanted to. This time, daughter would simply watch as her throat would be dry by now and all energy drained after shouting and protecting her mother from domestic violence. It was an unsaid rule laid down by the mind games played by the father that the daughter has to protect her mother during domestic fights at all costs. In exchange, mother would fulfill her educational needs, give her clothing and food and of course, the needed love and care. All these things would nourish the daughter in the right way and help her blossom into a person ready to become absolutely like her mother. When the time comes, she will be used exactly like her mother. Used for what? Used to feed her younger sister!!! In the exactly same way as she was fed. A vicious cycle, a cycle in which father had to just function as a demonic catalyst to keep the three ladies in control and work according to his plan. The whole strategy was planned out. Mother and the daughter were mere pawns.

At school, it was a different life for the daughter. There was fame. There was love showered upon by teachers. Mother made sure that her daughter was treated appropriately by landing into parent-teacher meetings and making her intentions clear to the teacher. At least somewhere her daughter should be treated well! If not home, then at school. The mother never had to do much of a hard work in achieving this goal of hers as the daughter was good enough to accomplish this goal herself. She being good at studies and fluent in English made her a star at school. The mother just did the goal polishing every time she came for the meetings at school.

Daughter just loved being at school. Being part of a school made her feel that she was a part of something huge, very huge. She felt as if she is the reason behind big changes happening in the world. This exaggerated feeling was nothing more than a big lie but with all the motivating speeches she delivered on school stage, it all seemed true. Everybody loved and admired her for who she was. Not at all like home where father used to scold her on every little thing. Eventually, she became the class prefect. That was her first big victory at school. As she continued to climb on the ladder of school fame, she finally became the school head girl. Not to forget, the best thing about her was her voice. She was the one who said the before lunch prayer on stage and students repeated after her. These small and big accomplishments made her overcome the trials and tribulations of domestic violence faced at home. In no way this school fame was directed towards achieving something grand in the future. After all, it was her part time job to study. She did not study well to become something huge. She did all this because these acts of victory gave her strength to endure the excruciating pain at home. When a water droplet falls on a rusted leaf, it heals the leaf. What if there are many water droplets falling on the same rusted leaf?? It cannot make the leaf as fresh as new but can still make her better than before. The school achivements worked in the same way as these little water droplets for the disturbed mind and heart of the daughter.

CHAPTER FOUR

The sweet admirer

Daughter had a sweet admirer at school. He used to sit just behind him. As and when the bench rotation rules and sitting arrangement would disappear, the sweet admirer would sit with the daughter. She would also not mind at all because she loved the fact that somebody liked her so much. She enjoyed all the attention he would give her.

Daughter took admission in a missionary convent school near her house in fifth standard. The sweet admirer took admission into her class in eighth standard. As the daughter was always busy during the school hours performing her duties, she had no time to notice the newcomer. The sweet admirer caught the daughter's attention for the very first time when one day he was waiting for his school van after the school got over. Waiting silently? No, not at all! He was one mischievous fellow. He would play with school juniors in the empty classrooms till the school van came. When the daughter first noticed her, he was in his Saturday white uniform sitting slightly tilted on one of the classroom tables near the window. He was smiling and giggling along with all his juniors who were sitting on the other nearby tables. It felt as if a prankish leader is enjoying lazily with his fellow disciples after the morning sermon had finished.

Daughter also went in the second shift of school bus. So, she also had plenty of time to have some conversation with the newcomer. But she was not interested in any sort of chat with him as she was basking in the glory of her school extempore victory today. She had just accidentally entered into the same classroom. As soon as the newcomer saw her coming into the classroom with a medal around her neck, he commented "Kuch talent hamaare liye bhi chhodh do J" Well, that was true. The daughter was exceptionally talented. She was good at studies; held the most prestigious positions at school; had a soulful voice; won medals in extempore, declamations and debates. The only thing in which she used to fail was sports. She never won but she enjoyed playing basketball, badminton, volleyball and bowling which eventually became her favourite game. Above all, she was good at heart.

The statement "Kuch talent hamaare liye bhi chhodh do J" was the first step towards admiration. As the time passed, this admiration only grew. The newcomer became the sweet admirer. Everyone admired the daughter but he was different. His daily admiration brought a subtle touch into her life which soothed her. He flirted with every school girl thus becoming the ultimate casanova. But with the daughter, he was different, he was much more genuine. More than admiration, respect thrived in his heart for her. It was visible in his eyes. This was not the case with other school girls.

Daughter was very fond of the sweet admirer but she never showed him. She knew that all this is not her real life. Her reality is the one which she sees at home. She constantly reminded herself of this. She always held her emotions for the boy because she knew that all this is like a dream which would fade away anyday. What will be left is sheer domestic violence caused by her father. That is her true identity which does not allow her the liberty to be expressive about things like love, care and admiration. Her hands were so full dealing with the brutal ways of his father that she did not have the ability to appreciate the sweet admirer in full measure. Her emotionless nature also came from fear. She was afraid that her problems will consume the boy as well if she lets her heart open to him. The best thing of her life used to be in front of him every day but she never took the risk to admire him back.

Class lectures were a serious affair, at least for the daughter and most of her class. The sweet admirer would mostly eat his lunch with friends if the lecture used to be boring. He and his gang would sit in the last two benches and stealthily enjoy eating each other's lunch. Three hours experimental labs were relatively chill compared to the class lectures. Experiments used to get over in one hour or so and students would be free after that. The sweet admirer would utilize this time by praising the daughter to his female friends. What a boy!

CHAPTER FIVE

The heart crush

The sweet admirer liked class maths topper! This news crushed daughter's heart. The most beautiful feeling of her life was suddenly taken away from her. For some strange reason, she believed that all the love and care of sweet admirer was meant only for her. He being the class casanova lingering around every girl for attention, talking to them, flirting with them, was more than enough to annoy her. Now this affair with the maths topper! She was furious and crushed at the same time. The boy's credibility became a very doubtful affair for her.

She wanted to go straight to the boy and slap him. But why? Why is she getting so angry? The boy never promised her to give anthing more than admiration. She also never reciprocated back in a way that would pave way for love. Whenever the sweet admirer would come to her during lunch time for a little chat, the daughter would keep ignoring the conversation. She was just too afraid that the boy might see her eyes and get to know her real feelings. Feelings of love, compassion and longing for the boy but who knew that this jerk will start liking somebody else.

Everything was going according to the daughter's plan. The sweet admirer liked somebody else now. This meant that she has to no longer worry about holding her feelings back. She believed that once the boy's attention will be diverted towards another girl, he would no longer bother her. This way she would also get some time to get over the boy. Her feelings for him would also fade away. She will be back to her normal self. This never happened! The longingness and the pain only increased with time, no matter what.

Love stories of the sweet admirer and her girlfriend (the maths topper) had taken the whole class by storm. They had become the talk of the town. As he was very social unlike the daughter, he had many friends in class who would talk about his love story and make him more popular. His crazy friends would cook up stories that how he managed to impress the most beautiful and the wittiest girl of his class. These stories made the daughter much more furious. Steam used to come out of her ears listening to this drama. Thank god she had lot of responsibilities at school which kept her busy and diverted. Otherwise she would have definitely killed the boy for liking somebody else.

Again why? Why was the daughter so furious when this is what she wanted? Perhaps, she wanted the boy to intrude her heart and churn love out of her dispassionate soul. Was the boy intelligent enough to understand this? No. Was all this so easy to do? No. Daughter knew this. That's why she did not hold any grudge against him. It was only pure love in her heart. But still, she wanted him to wait. She wanted him to stay a little longer. Who knows, the constant appreciation by the boy which showed that he cared about her would have inclined the daughter towards him! After all, true love stays, stays and tries to soothe the companion till the last breath, even if everything is against them. This is what daughter believed. She believed that if the boy truly loved her, he would not have given up on her so easily. This realization caused the heart crush.

CHAPTER SIX

Sab mithyaa hai

The only good thing of daughter's life had gone. Everthing seemed falsehood. A strong sense of detachment crept into her heart and mind. Gradually, she realized that nothing was hers. No one was hers. Father was too busy setting house rules and controlling people living in the house. Mother was too busy doing her job and rebelling father. The sweet admirer was engaged with his new love. What was left for her? Where was it? Nowhere. The only thing she had was her studies and her love for competitions like extempore, declamation etc. Nothing else.

She absorbed herself completely into studies and interesting school activities. Everything else used to happen in front of her but nothing affected her. This is because she has stopped expecting anything from anybody. She accepted the fact that nothing is going to change at home even if she dies because of all the violence. She also came into terms with the fact that she was nothing more than a friend for the sweet admirer.

She started speaking very less in the class. Her interaction in the class became very limited. Be it experimental labs or classrooms, she kept herself engaged in her work. Nothing else mattered to her. What else was she supposed to do? The morning and evening doses of domestic violence never failed to happen everyday. The only little relief was this school boy who also now went to somebody else.

Avoiding was the key for her now. She used to avoid the boy during the lunch hours. Everybody used to sit together for lunch and talk about different things. But she used to get up as soon as she finished eating food and run away in the name of school duties, even when she did not have one. She felt so strongly for the boy that it could be seen in her eyes. She dreaded this fact! That's why she never gave boy the chance to interact with her much. By chance if the boy looks in her eyes and gets to know her real feelings, it would be a disaster for both. Therefore, at lunch time, when students get ample time to talk to each other and share stories, she never gave him the chance to talk to her much and kept avoiding him.

Why did he do so? If she meant nothing to her, why did he bring pictures of his elder brother's wedding and showed to her. Why did he share his personal life with him? After the school hours, when both the daughter and the sweet admirer used to wait for their buses, they used to spend time talking with each other as their friendship grew. The boy would do memorable stuff during that time. For instance, once the daughter was buying ice cream from the seller standing just in front of the school, as she was taking out some change from her spectacle box (the girl used to keep the change in her spectacle box! What a girl!), the boy came running from behind and swiftly passed beside her. Ice cream would have fallen had he been a little more closer to her. The wedding picture incident mentioned above was also the one which took place after the school hours waiting for their buses. The boy very fondly brought pictures to show how beautiful her sister-in-law was. The daughter was so madly in love with the boy that she would have praised any picture he showed to her. In this case, the boy's sister-in-law was really praiseworthy, so she appreciated it in full measure. Everything was so wonderful. Why did he ruin it? This is all what she wanted to ask. But to whom? And why? The boy did not promise her anything. She never reciprocated back in a way which would mean anything more than a friend to him. Why this uneasiness in her mind? Even if the boy feels something for her, will she be comfortable enough to accept it at this point of time? No. She knows that right now she does not possess the ability to handle and nourish a complex emotion like love when she has so much to tackle at home. Then, why this chaos in her mind? As the daughter was looking for answers to these questions, her mind accepted the fact that whatever is happening is best for now. Eventually, she gave up the mind battle and chose to go with the flow. As one surrenders to the circumstances, life feels empty and detachment crepts in.

CHAPTER SEVEN

The ultimate training of being a homemaker

Father had started a secret school of building homemakers. That was the main foundation of domestic violence. And the only student admitted in this school was the daughter. She had no other choice. Mother was too busy getting promoted and earning more and more money to fulfill the needs of the family. Younger sister was too small. Father was in no mood to be the better half in true sense and share the household responsibilities with the mother. Irrespective of being employed or not, he never ever took the household responsibilities wholeheartedly. It was always something which was a huge burden on him and like most males in the world, he felt an identity crisis while performing these duties. Easiest solution in such a situation was the daughter.

It was very easy for father to put every other household duty on the daughter. She was docile and too young to understand the intricacies of life, so she can be dictated. She wants to avoid domestic violence at all costs, so she can be dictated. If she does not want to perform all these duties, she does not have any other resort left, so she can be dictated. Morover, she can be scolded to any extent at all times without any interruption because the mother will not be at home before 5 PM (5 PM might extend to 8 PM at times) to stop the father. Life has always been about the mother and her job. Clock of the daughter's house worked according to the mother's timetable and no matter how weary the house was, it was always the responsibility of the daughter to gather everything up at house. Nothing could be expected out of father except dictatorship on the daughter to keep everything prim and proper and in working condition at home.

The most pricking moment of all times used to be in the evenings when the mother used to come from the college (she was working in a college) like a guest to a home where the daughter is functioning like a pro-homemaker dusting sofas and folding clothes. Amidst all this, the mother would childishly scold the daughter to stop dusting and cleaning every nook and corner of the house as if she is not at all aware of the reason behind this! Now, here comes the ultimate guest, the so called father, who gets up from sleep (he has ample time to sleep because most of the time he is unemployed) once the mother lands in and appreciates her for conquering the world. Of course, why will he not appreciate her, after all, she is bringing money into the family. Father's life was sorted, one lady earning money and the other cleaning house. What a happy life! This would not have been possible without his famous coaching classes of homemaking. This is because if he does not keep training and monitoring the daughter at every step about her household duties, house would be in chaos. And if house would not be well-managed, it would refrain the mother from concentrating fully at her job. So, who is the ultimate hero? Of course, the demonic father.

The most important lesson of this homemaker training was "folding clothes". The precision and punctuality expected in this work by the father was nothing less than that needed in cracking a national level exam. Every evening, the daughter had to pick up clothes hanging in the balcony and fold them in a way which would be a reflection of an efficient homemaker. Initially, in order to make clear that this evening activity needs to be followed like a ritual, the father used to hold fights with the entire family (the mother, the daughter, the younger sibling and the grandfather) to make his intentions clear. The whole agenda of his fighting would be to teach the daughter to fold clothes on time! He would make the daughter realize that she is of no use if she cannot perform these household duties on time. The mother, on the other hand, would ask the daughter to rebel him by putting across points which would prove her calibre like getting good grades in class, being the class topper etc. These fights used to be endless. But how these fights minimized?? Was there an end to such conversations? Yes and no. Yes, because slowly the daughter learnt that no matter what, she has to pick up the clothes from the balcony every evening and fold them with utmost accuracy. She accepted the fact that this is her duty and not at all of her mother. In fact, with time, she also came into terms with the fact that the sarees and suits which her mother used to change after coming back home from work are her responsibility. She has to very precisely fold those sarees and give her best in doing so. Oh! Wow! What all expectations from a school going kid. Why these expectations? Why not? After all, the mother is always busy with her workplace phonecalls or even more important, relatives and friends phonecalls. She has been working all day long in college, she must be needing some free time to chat and gossip on phone or do work. This is all fair. This was the kind of mentality which the father supported and tried to engrave it in his children's mind as well. The one who earns money can never go wrong and he/she must be obeyed. The father's action supported this kind of belief which had to be followed by the daughter as well. She had no other choice.

No, because due to any reason, if the daughter fails to fold the evening clothes, the father would again start the whole fight which would go on endlessly until it gets imprinted into the daughter's mind for many years to come that how big a mistake she has committed. It seemed as if this activity determined the character of the daughter and how well she will perform in her life. Every character blame used to thrown at her by the frustrated father for not performing the duty. All this had a huge impact on the daughter's mental health because gradually, she lost the ability to rebel even for the right things in life and succumbed to the circumstances. Most importantly, she developed for such precautionary attitude for such small things in life that there came a point when achieving bigger things was no longer on her mind. All she was concerned about was these mundane things in house. Now, what's say, was she not becoming an ideal homemaker? A sense of fear developed in her mind regarding these small household things which used to bother her every now and then like is would bother any fully devoted homemaker. All the traits of an ideal homemaker started growing in her with time. These traits grew to such an extent that there were times when during afternoon sleeps, the daughter would blabber about taking out washing machine clothes. She used to have such anxieties about unfinished household works.

What is so wrong in all this? The wrong part is that she was not suppose to experience all this at such an early age. People may say that and they say it all the time that the silver lining is that she has learnt taking good care of the house at such an early age which is very good for her future. But the question here is not about learning, it is about the way of learning. Everytime some work is to be done at home, the daughter should do it because the mother is at job and the father is too busy in dictating the girl. The wrong part is that she was not suppose to learn all this in such traumatic ways. The wrong part is that these small things have been embedded to such an extent in her mind that is no longer has the space to hold something more beautiful, more innovative. The problem is that she was not suppose to learn all this to such an extent which makes her realize that there is no point for a girl to have a career because then, she would be doing everything on her own, be it job or housework. If she is lucky enough, she will have a daughter just like her to take care of the house when she becomes working. But she does not want this to repeat! So, what is she suppose to do? How is she suppose to react to such circumstances? These unanswered questions in her mind are the problem. It is these unanswered questions which stop her from flourishing professionally because all the effort seems to be in vain. The problem is the fear that has grown in her mind, the fear to do small things right, the fear which has now become a barrier in her growth.

CHAPTER EIGHT

What have I done wrong?

'What have I done wrong?' asked the daughter to herself, every time she was tortured in the name of domestic violence. At times, she used to cry for hours at odd hours without any specific reason. The mental trauma she went through due to the strained relationship of her parents used to find a vent through her eyes. There was no one to listen, no one to help. When she needed the help the most, no one was there. Tears used to flow endlessly. The best and the worst part of these god damn tears is that they never care about the place and time. When emotions become too much to handle, they just flow. Same used to happen with the daughter. Be it school, be it home, tears would flow down continuously whenever she got reminded of the stuff she never wants to remember.

Nothing changed between parents. Everything between them just grew worse. What changed was the nature of the daughter's tears. Initially, whenever flood of tears would flow down her eyes, they would be red hot holding fire in them. These tears would be little shots of flame and anguish demanding action, demanding revenge, demanding justice. There would be shouting amd howling alongwith these cries of pain. There would be times when the mother would be cooking in the kitchen and the daughter would sit on the floor repenting and crying and scraming in pain, the mental pain which she no longer wants to tolerate. But in life, there is no midway. You can be in this way for a while but for not very long. Sooner or later, you have to be all in or all out. There was no doubt that the daughter wanted to be all out of this situation as she could not take it anymore. But she could not. Neither that day nor today, because the mother was not ready. Neither that day nor today! Slowly and gradually, this realization seeped into the mind of the daughter as she observed the mother. She painfully accepted the truth that the mother would defend her and be on her side to protect her from the father but would never leave him. So, now what choice did the daughter have? To be all in or all out? Of course, to be all in. Why was the daughter being punished for a toxic relationship between her parents? Thus asked the daughter to herself 'What have I done wrong?' This question remained. The pain remained. The nature of the tears altered. Unlike earlier, they became a calmer version of themselves. No fire, no revenge, just the patient remorseful acceptance of the reality : this is what the daughter's tears expressed now. There were still bouts of anxiety and depression in the daughter's life which took the shape of tears flowing down her eyes. But now these tears were wrapped in a shroud of numbness devoid of hope and expectations.

The daughter, the father and the mother: all three lying on the bed at night to finally sleep. Suddenly, the father started trying to beat the daughter for trying to study so much and the mother trying to act as a defence by stopping the hands of the father. As a response, the daughter closed her eyes and curled up like a newborn baby to protect herself from the beating. Thus asked the daughter to herself 'What have I done wrong?' Such episodes of domestic violence haunted her every now and then. The daughter used to understand that all these misdoings of the father are a result of his frustration on his job, on his wife, on his life. She accepted this and had complete sympathy with him but was it right to hold one little girl responsible for everything? Was it right to vent out all his frustration on a little girl by pointing out flaws in every little act of hers and scold her every now and then for no reason? Thus asked the daughter 'What have I done wrong?'.

The mother defended the daughter, the mother protected the daughter but was too afraid to understand the psychology of the father and make him a person he wants to be. The mother was too afraid to do that. Instead, she surrendered herself completely to the father and took the burden of all his duties. For her, this was the solution of all the domestic violence and chaos. What was the main duty of the father to be taken care of ? It was feeding the children by being the breadwinner of the house. The mother took up that duty. The father never wanted that, he instead wanted the support of his wife in being the main hero of the house. But it never happened. This is because the mother started earning to escape all the domestic violence in the house which also gave her the side privileges which the father had desired. These side privileges included the love of the daughter, good name and fame in the society. All this caused more and more pain in the father's life thus resulting into more and more violence in the house. The father was busy causing trouble in the house and the mother was busy escaping the father through her job. Who was the ultimate sufferer? The daughter. Thus asked the daughter to herself 'What have I done wrong?'. The daughter would be home by 2 PM from school and she would become the victim of the father's disappointments and anger.

What kind of life was this for the daughter, where her mother was a very self-sufficient lady but the house was never a happy place to live? What kind of life was this for the daughter where there was a false image in the society that her mother is well-established but actually, the reality was that it is the father's constant fear that serves as the fuelling factor in the mother's life? It is this fear in the heart and the mind of the mother which helps her to the best at work. Fear is the foundation. Toxicity is the result, This toxicity was evident in the lives of each and everyone living in the house. In the father's case, it was evident in his anger on every little problem. In the mother's case, it was visible in defending herself during the fights with the father. All this had to be born by the daughter. Thus asked the daughter to herself 'What have I done wrong?'

CHAPTER NINE

Welcome to the world of toxic growth

Growth governed by fear and anger can never be good. It is the growth governed by love and passion which leads to boundless happiness and success. The father never understood this. He wanted toxic growth for the mother. Money poured in, goodwill poured in, fame poured in but it took away the daughter's desire to grow and flourish. Her good deeds only became a way to escape from the house violence and nothing more than that. A dispassionate feeling crept into her heart and mind for success and prosperity.

Everything the mother did was governed by one core belief : the fear of the father, the fear of his beating, the fear that he might beat her daughters. This is toxic growth. Her morning routine had lots of yellings and shoutings of the father. Until the time she would not step out of the house for her work, violence would continue. The father would sometimes yell at her behavior, sometimes because of the food, sometimes because of the daughter's behavior. Reason could be anything. And unaware of the tactics of the father, the mother would yell back till the last minute and leave the house for work. This is toxic growth. Do you know why it is toxic? Because the whole day, the primary thought in the mother's mind is violence and the other feelings (whether good or bad) of the day become secondary. Do you know why it is toxic? Because this way, the father had taken full control over the mother's mind and could trigger violence at any time of the day once she is back from work. Do you know why it is toxic? Because it is not even a growth, it is enslavery.

Amidst this toxicity, the daughter grew. She absorbed every bit of it and thus refuses to grow professionally! She knows that the history would repeat and the same would happen with her. She knows the whole mechanism by which the father manufactures professionally successful ladies! She has seen her mother become one and she does not want to grow professionally the same way. If anyone were to ask the daughter that how a toxic growth takes place, she would be able to explain the whole process line by line. Toxic growth gives you money, power, fame but the bondage never ends. The bondage is the fear embedded deep into the heart of the concerned person. This fear can be of any person or a particular circumstance. In this case, it was of the father.

How did the father operate his toxic growth process? It would start by breaking the person emotionally, physically, spiritually. He would do everything which would break you so that a newer stronger version of yourself would come up. He would fight endlessly with you, whenever he would get time. He would, of course, not disturb you during your office hours because that is the time when you are earning money for him! If situation does not go according to his plan, then he would take the liberty to disturb you during that time as well but it is very rare. In the morning, he would fight with you until you don't leave for work and as soon as you land up in the house again in the evening, he would start the fight again. Why would he do so? Again, the same logic, he wants to be the primary thing on your mind. Basically, he unintentionally teaches you detachment from every single thing on this planet and finally, the soul thing which will matter to you is his scolding and beating. So, you see, he becomes the new god! But does anybody has the right to take the place of the superpower sitting above? No, not at all. The father is a human being like the mother or the daughter and if he wants to become god, he has to achieve that status through his good karma. Controlling and manipulating the mother and the daughter for his own benefits is not the right thing to do.

So, continuing with the explanation of the toxic process, the father would completely embed his fear into the person. That's why, the mother was always fearsome. But then how was she always smiling and laughing, enjoying every moment? Why did she not go to a mental hospital due to so much stress? Here's the trick. Like a bait to a fish, the father would arouse feelings of greed into the person for luxury which the earned money would buy. He did the same with the mother. Mother, like any other person, liked it. After being broken in every way, when you start afresh with a new identity (from a housewife to a college professor, then director), even a small achievement would fill you with gratitude. Gratitude comes in, money comes in, desire to shop for luxury is planted by the father. Everything becomes positive. What's next? The father would stay near you at all times in the house, looking at you, observing you, as soon as you deviate from your path of serving him and the family, he would scold you and beat you, if necessary, beat you to death and then make you live again! Who does all this? The father does all this. He enjoys this game. He played this game with the mother but the daughter does not like this game. This is what irritates the father! The father is not getting his next catch, as planned by him.

The daughter refuses to grow this way. She demands healing first because all this has taken a toll on her mental health. During the toxic growth of her mother, it was she who had to always be the bigger person and stop the fights between her parents. Even if she was injured during the fights, she had to make peace with it. She always had to increase her patience level to accept the injustice happening at her house. All this caused mental injuries to her. If this is how a person blossoms into its fullest potential, then she does not want to progress at all. Alongwith the mother, she also became detached from everything existing on this planet because all she could hear was the father's bullshit sermons all day long, meant to break; mould and reform the mother. Fear is the foundation, fear is the top, fear is the bottom, fear is omnipresent in this growth process; so she denies to accept this. Therefore, whatever the daughter did was out of a dispassionate feeling which gave birth to amazing achievements because she was persisitent and hardworking in her efforts. The question is, how long can the daughter escape the toxic growth treatment of the father? How long can she continue on her own? To know what happens next, keep reading.

CHAPTER TEN

Freedom or no freedom?

This question haunts the mind of the daughter every single day of her life. She is living in a state of confusion. This confusion is her biggest punishment of being the daughter of her mother and father. She lives in a state where nothing feels right. Moving forward in career and blossoming in an individual with an identity of her won feels wrong. Staying where she is and being a mere observer feels wrong. What is she suppose to do? Whether she wants to be the part of the kind of freedom bestowed by her father or not? This question keeps reeling in her brain every single minute of her life.

What is she suppose to choose? If she surrenders to the chaotic growth process of her father, she will lose all her self-respect. She will never be able to look in the mirror again. If she stays where she is, life does not and cannot work for her this way. Because then there is society who wants answer for everything. Why are you not working? When your mother is such a professional lady achieving new heights of success each day, why are you not working towards your goal with the same passion and grit? Don't you want to change your fate for good be setting a new identity for yourself? All these questions will start pouring in for her is she just chooses to stay where she is. Moreover, there is financial aspect which needs to be taken care of.

This is the biggest bane for the family! Father has given freedom to the ladies of the house which doesn't feel like freedom. Haha! This is the biggest loss for the father as well. The mother is anyways happy for what she has got, at least this is what is felt by the daughter. At times, she would cry, she would defend, she would fight, she would shout, she would howl. But the end result? The end result is always about submitting to the vicious wishes of the father. Do you know why? Because there is clarity in her heart and mind, which the daughter can clearly see in her eyes. Clarity which comes in after years of realization that no matter what, she cannot escape the cruel doings of the father. Giving up is not ok, giving up and not facing the circumstances headstrong is not ok, but sometimes you need to break the year long ties which damage you mentally and physically. The mother never understood this.

Who was being damaged the most out of everything going on? The daughter. The mother had gone through the ruthless growth process invented by the so called father for once. But the daughter had to go through it twice, if she continues to even live. And she is not ready for it. She demands healing, she demands justice for the mental wounds which her parents have caused her. She is not ok with the kind of freedom her father would give her. She is not ok with the kind of freedom which would damage her self-respect, her pride, her feminine side. She is not ok with the kind of freedom which is basically not a freedom at all. It is just a form of enslavery where you get to breathe just because you bring money, fame and power for the house.

The whole point of the daughter is that what is the point of having a freedom where there is so much of confusion about the fact that whether we are free or not? Is this freedom or not? Or are we just being used in exchange of some money, food and daily luxury? There is a male in the house who beats you every now and then, makes his fear the biggest agenda of your life, in fact the only agenda of your life and helps you earn money in return of that. Wow! What a freedom, where the keys of your brain and heart are with the father. And you can do nothing about it.

Girls, do not give the keys of your brain and heart to anybody else. Because then you are free but not free. Choose your fights diligently. Be strong. Be selective in your fights. Most importantly, snip off the ties from your life which do not free you the way you want. Be the one who chooses to step back, think, analyse and work accordingly. It is nothing wrong in stepping back for your own good. This is what the story of the daughter tells you. It inspires you to be free free.

Of what use is this freedom of the mother to the daughter? This freedom does not inspire her. This freedom has only given her pain, more pain and more pain. Being in the shackles of the father's toxic growth process for so very long, the mother has even forgotten the meaning of true freedom. Thank god, the daughter has not. She is not expert either but still, there is a confusion in her mind. This confusion is a hope that the daughter still believes that true freedom is no the one given by her father to the mother. The confusion that the freedom given by the father to the mother is actually a freedom or not is the testimony of the fact that she wants a new sunrise. It is an indication that she wants a new path to be paved where the meanings of the freedom given to women are redefined. If this confusion is gone and she compleltely surrenders to the brutal ways of his father just because then she will be having a job; earning money and having fame and power (which is all good for someone to stand in the society), That day would be the biggest loss of her life. That is the day she will lose herself completely. Because that will be the day when she would have completely forgotten that how a true freedom feels like. The keys of her brain and heart would be in the hands of the father and she would only live for some luxury items and shopping. No heart, no soul, no thinking of her own. Identity but no identity. So, let the confusion: Freedom or no freedom? sustain and give rise to new beginnings.

CHAPTER ELEVEN

How does it feel to take stand for one's own self? How do we do it?

Avoiding domestic violence at all costs became such an important thing that the daughter forgot to give importance to any other thing. The daughter forgot to form her own beliefs and stand for them. The only thing which mattered to her was escaping domestic violence. It was either domestic violence or nothing : such became her life.

At the age of 25 when she started earning money and the parents wanted to suddenly become the happiest person on this earth (because she has earned a job and can pay for her bills and most importantly, the family's bills), she does not how to react. Because she does not know that what does a person feel like when the family becomes happy and domestic violence is gone. She does not know how that what is a person suppose to do when the father stops blaming the child for everything going wrong in his life. Her brain had rotten because of all the nuisance that had happened in her life. She does not know what are her beliefs, what are the things which are important to her, what is she suppose to do with her new kind of life when her brain is not able to process this.

The brain had gone numb, completely numb. She now realized that the domestic violence of her life has become such an integral part of her life that it now functions as a drug for her. You don't want to take it but you need it. The soul seems empty without it. The day feels incomplete without it. She wants to leave it but how? Throughout her life what she has done is saving her mother from father's beating, saving herself from father's beating, standing beside her mother at all times, defending her till the last breath. She has been so busy saving her mother from the father that she does not know anything else know. Whatever was right for the mother as right for her because she had to save the family. She had to be such a good emotional supporter and her follower in every way that there is no room for the father to harm them. In the process, she did nor form her beliefs. And now when her parents give her the chance to live a fully happy independent life, she does not how to do it. Because she know that the trauma of domestic violence is not going to end. The father will find new issues to fight the same way he fights with the mother for every single thing. She know that her life is going to be more hell and there is no even a single comforting thing in her journey to hell. The mother atleast has the privilege to buy the luxury items for herself and go for shopping clothes to release her stress. The daughter knows that she does not have this privilege as well. She has no reason to go forward in life except the reason that she wants to write this book. She has absolutely no reason. But why? Why does she also not go on a shopping spree every now and then like the mother does? Why does she also not enjoy her journey through the hell by taking care of the needs of her younger sibling (and by finding a way to buy some things for herself in the name of younger sister, like the mother used to do with the daughter)? Because she know that going by her will is going against the mother's will. And this is not something she is allowed to do. Throughout her life, she has been such an ardent follower of her mother's beliefs that she no longer has the privilege to live on her own terms. If the mother likes the top or t-shirt with flowers on it, the daughter has to buy that one, no matter what. She does not and cannot go for a blue plain t-shirt instead.

Everybody needs a reason to move forward in life, rather a purpose which gives meaning to their life. The daughter has been that one reason in the mother's life. And the daughter knows this. She does not blame the mother for being so insanely caring for her. What else a married woman suppose to do when her husband and everyone in the family leaves her? From where is a person suppose to find strength when he/she cannot trust anybody? The person finds strength in the new born who defines her future decisions because it is for the new born that the person still wants to go on striving. Fulfilling the needs of the new born becomes the foundation of all decisions. And in doing so, intentionally or unintentionally, the person finds a healing himself/ herself. When you take your baby in your hands, it heals you. It gives new meaning to your life. As the baby grows, he/ she grows through emotional traumas but when you sit with them and wipe their tears, somewhere you heal yourself as well. When your sleep with your baby at night tightly hugging him/ her, your forget all your worries and want to live more. Your forget whatever abuses your husband has given you during the day and you want to hang in there. This is the power of love. It wants you to be a better version of yourself for your loved ones. Al this becomes so much more magical when the child reciprocates in the same way with equal warmth and affection. It doubles the strength of the parent. All this becomes much more cherishing when the child understands the pain and the sacrifice of the parent and supports them by loving and respecting them. This is exactly what the daughter did for her mother. She understood her mother's pain caused to her due to the daily domestic violence in the house and she never let her shatter. There were times when the mother could not even muster the courage to step out of the house as she used to be completely shattered after huge domestic fights. Then, the daughter used to provide her the stability she needed at that time. All this came at a cost. The daughter now does not know how to live without the violence. Now, the daughter does not know that what are her beliefs. She only knows her mother's beliefs. Even in the deep corner of her heart, she truly cares for something and stand for them, she does not how to do it. She only knows how to stand for her mother's beliefs.

CHAPTER TWELVE

Keeping them enriched

A very very tedious task for the daughter which needed constant hard work, patience and perseverance. Keeping the wrecked life of her parents all patched up together somehow, a very tedious task. She did it, for the sake of her mother, for the sake of the family. After of all, all of them including herself needed some good things in life to survive, to keep going. But the sad part is that her parents don't realize this work of hers which she has been doing from the day she has been able to feel the pain of domestic violence in the house.

Why to call this enrichment when it is basically providing some healing to the parents through the good achivements of the daughter? Because her achivements would have been nothing without the hard work and good achivements of the mother. The mother has always been number one in bringing happiness into home. There is no denying in this. But this is not the point here. The point is that do these parents even realize that what sacrifices the daughter has made these many years to just be able to stick around them? The father has always been brutal. The only thing he knew best in life was to suck life out of everything and anything. He had always had an extracting nature. The mother has always been busy defending herself and protecting her daughter from his beating. Her efforts have been phenomenal. But that does not mean at all that daughter did not give her one hundred percent to be able to survive in the house where only domestic violence has been the way of living since ages.

It is true that the mother's professional success was always a matter of utmost happiness in the house because it brought more and more money into the family. As it relieved the burden of earning from the father's shoulders, he was always very pleased to hear all this stuff and celebrate. Then, his children use to join in. But the grief which came along with all this happiness could become unbearable at times for the family because all these things led to sheer domestic violence as well. How? Why? Due to the father's growing uncertainities about his own progress, about his own job, about his own personality. So, basically, everything the mother achieved professionally used to be void in terms of happiness spread in the family.

What were the other healings in the house? These other healings were the daughter's achivements. When she used to come first in her class, it used to be a healing for the family. When she used to come first in extempores and debates, it used to be a healing. When she used to come first in dance competitions, it used to be a healing. When at parent teacher meetings the teachers used to praise her for all the good work she did, it used to be healing. When she became the class prefect, that was a healing. When she became the school head girl, that was a healing. When she understood the pains and sacrifices of her parents to earn money and behaved like a good girl by demanding no firecrackers on a Diwali night, that was also for their happiness. It was all as little addons to their existing happiness. They never had much to be happy about but whatever was there, the daughter added to that by performing her bit.

Dear readers, you know what? When you perform these kind of enrichments for someone, even if they were your parents, they expect more. They expect something bigger and better coming there way. The daughter did not realize this earlier. She did not see this coming. Her parents never realized that making these small contributions in the family through her achivements and spreading happiness was difficult enough for her after living in such a dysfunctional family. They did not realize even once that living in a family where domestic violence is the only thing going on throughout the day, it must have been really hard for the daughter to achieve even what she has achieved. They were always so busy resolving their own issues and ego problems with each other. They never go time to pay heed to anything else. They expect more and more from the daughter in terms of better job, better car, better paycheck, better everything. What about her mental health? What about her choices? Nobody asks her that what is going to keep her enriched? She worked hard in school so that she can see smile on the mother's face (somtimes on the father's face as well). She really hoped that her small achivements at school will really make the parents forget about their messed up life for a couple of minutes until they again enter into their dark mental caves of domestic violence. All this really happened but they should have realized that all this takes a toll on the daughter as she is doing her best to stick around. Most importantly, they should not have asked for more. All this has been hard enough for the daughter! They should have released that on time.

CHAPTER THIRTEEN

All energy drained, nothing more to offer

The daughter is drained completely now. She has nothing more to offer to her parents. Domestic violence in her life has consumed her totally, in and out. Her sentiments are drained, her ability to outshine others is drained, her voice to stand for herself is drained, her voice to stand for others is drained. She has been clapperclawed completely. Domestic violence of the house has eaten her.

This is what twenty five years of rigorous domestic violence does to you. It murders you in and out. It paralyses you completely. You want to get rid of it but you cannot. It did the same to the daughter. The life ahead of her seemed void to her. Throughout these years, domestic violence has so profound in her life that she spent all her energy overcoming it and now she has nothing to give to her parents. She wants replenishment.

Till the time she was not earning, her studies were the escape to the domestic violence. Her studies gave her the reason to be alive. Alongwith that, she performed all her household duties like a good daughter to the mother. But now, her studies have become equally painful to her because this is how she is earning her money presently and since the money is very important to the father, he has brutally entered into this one segment which was left untouched by him. In fact, the mother has also entered because money is an important thing. This is what the daughter does not like at all. She wants to run away.

The only thing where she could be her ownself and enjoyed the freedom of expression was taken by the father. Now, she has nothing to live for. This entire time she stayed away from the money calculations of the house because she knew that it is one of the major reasons of domestic violence in the house. But now, knowingly or unknowingly, she has to be a part of it and of the domestic violence as well. And all this has already started. The thing she feared the most has happened. Can't she defend herself ? After all, she is not a baby. Everybody has to fight for themselves. No, she cannot fight because she neither has the intention nor the energy to do the same.

The reasons of the domestic violence in the house, the main topics which have been the bone of contention between her parents have taken away the very intention from her. When the intention to move forward in life is taken away from you, what else is left there to loose? It means that you have lost the battle. She knows that if she starts earning money (which she has started by the way), she will have to go through the same trials and tribulations which her mother went through. She will also have to pointlessly and endlessly argue with the father on vague topics, she will also have to pacify the ego of the father which would be hurt wthout no valid reason just because she has started earning. Not only this, on weekends, she will have to spend the whole day getting beatings from the father, like the mother got, because it is the favourite weekend pastime of the father. Yes, it is the favourite pastime of the father to beat the working ladies of the house. According to him, it keeps them in his control. This is the way he makes clear to the working ladies of the house that what is their actual place and where do they actually belong : in his feet. But alas! All her defensive energy and beliefs have drained fighting for the mother, protecting the mother when she was the sole earning member of the family. Everyday, slowly and gradually, with each fight happening at her house, the daughter lost all she had, in the name of stopping the chaos.

Oh God, help the daughter. The domestic violence of the house had led to a state of painc and confusion in the mother's mind. Although she used to function like any other normal person, go out and work but the state of panic used to be there. Until she used to recover from one bout of panic, other used to come up in the form of other domestic fight with the father. Who used to calm her down? Who used to make her feel well so that she can again function the next day? It was the daughter. Therefore, these twenty five years of extreme care for the mother has made her a person who wants to always be there for her mother. She does not want to earn herself because then she wont be able to properly take care of the mother. The frame of balance which the daughter-mother duo had formed was being broken by the father himself and hence, the daughter was worried. The daughter was worried now because she does not how to function now in this changed environment where she as well as the mother both will be the earning one and the father will be beating one. Who is going to save them? The younger daughter, haha, yes, very funny. This is one aspect of the story which worries the daughter and eats her each day. The other and the most important aspect is that she is exhausted of healing the mental and physical wounds of the mother which the father has caused her from time to time through domestic violence. She is tired seeing this injustice all these years where one is being damaged all the time and the wrongdoer is not being punished, instead, the third one has to come up to soothe the wounds of the damaged one with his/her love and compassion. What kind of setup is this? All this takes a lot energy, the daughter's parents need to understand this. And it is even more draining when you don't have anybody to fall back on. The daughter had nobody to fall back on. Everytime the father beat the mother, the daughter used to give her full legs massage. Everytime the father used to pull the mother brutally by catching her through her hair, the daughter used to heal her by oiling her hair and making her sleep. She used to give her healing head massage. From where does she get the energy to replenish? What keeps her going during such circumstances, when she has been equally involved in the fights and has been hurt? It is not as if the daughter does not want to take care of the mother. It has always been a pleasure for her to take care of the mother but taking care of "mother" is very different from taking care of "wounded mother". Everything becomes even more difficult when the wounds are just not physical, they are mental as well. The daughter is tired of all this and she has nothing more to offer. And in no circumstances, does she want her younger sibling to do the same what she did for her mother. Because the daughter knows what it takes to heal a wounded mother, someone whom you love so much and try to protect. There are no words to express this sheer pain. What is more inexpressible is the amount of power, love and compassion it takes to heal such wounds. It is absolutely very draining and she does not want her sister to go through the same suffering.

The very zeal to flourish, to grow, to be better professionally has been taken away from the daughter. This is how hard the domestic violence of the house has struck her. Zeal and enthusiasm to move forward in life gives you the energy to achieve your goals. If the zeal is not there, energy is automatically not there. The father should have really not followed the toxic way of progress wherein everything is smeared in domestic violence. It is this toxic process which has taken away everything from the daughter : her zeal, her beliefs, her energy and she has nothing more to offer to her parents and to the world. For now, going forward in life the way her mother did financially, leaving every problem going on in the house and achieving new goals, just doesn't feel right for the daughter. She demands healing. She wants to take a break. She wants to replenish all her energy which she has lost defending and protecting her mother from the father's domestic violence, defending and protecting herself from the father's beatings, doing all the household work (acting as a very good substitute of the mother at home) in panic and anxiety so that the father does not create a big issue out of these small things. Moreover, she needs time to think as to what matters to her the most after seeing so much in life at such an early age. She needs to think that after being part of the lives of such a couple who has shown her both sides of the coin (the sad unemployment through the father and the happy employment through the mother), which side she needs to stay on. She needs to find out that what gives meaning to her life.

CHAPTER FOURTEEN

It's now father's turn

Till now, till the age the daughter has not been earning formally through a proper job, she was the best confidante the mother could have. She had to be, she had no other choice. She had to function this way for the sake of the family. In a fight, you need to choose a side and stick by it at all times. This is what the daughter did. She chose the mother. Not only did she served as the best confidante, she was the mother's servant, mother's body massager, mother's hair oiler, mother's best replacement in the kitchen. She was everything the mother would have needed to go to work everyday without worrying about the house chores and she was also everything the mother would have needed to survive in a house which was filled with domestic violence dictated on the father's command. She was at the mother's beck and call everytime. Serving the mother in all these multiple ways took a toll on the daughter in every way, be it through her beliefs, be it through her change in nature. She had literally become someone who was there only to support her mother in whichever way she would have needed. And at this stage, after being this way for almost 10-15 years, you cannot expect a person to change in one night.

She had been made this way by the father. The father was the one who has been dictating the mother since time immemorial and in order to make things work the way he wanted, he needed the daughter to be the mother's closest everything : closest confidante, closest servant and what not. He took full advantage of a docile daughter who was ready to be anything for the house. He took full advantage. The father, through the mother, wanted to prepare such a person who is complete in every way. It has to be said, the father took full care of the mother!! Why did he want to do that? What was his selfish motive? It was the money. He wanted someone who can get the money in the house and then the happiness in the house. He wanted someone who can take over all his responsibilities which he should have performed as the only man of the house. In the process of achieving this biggest target of getting money earned from the mother, The father sacrificed the daughter completely.

The sole job of being there for the mother and in place of her consumed the daughter completely. It consumed her so much so that she lost the ability to think in any other direction. She lost the ability to think in the direction where the mother would be the one offering her the meal and she can enjoy the liberty to just sit on the dining table and eat. With time, all these liberties completely vanished from the daughter's life! The mother was always working and then more working and then more working. Her professional work kept on increasing with time until one day the daughter became her most apt replacement at kitchen. And as far as venting on the frustration of the father's doing was concerned, the daughter would give the mother company in this as well. After all both were equally annoyed and sad with the domestic violence doing of the father and the mother had to compulsorily vent out this frustration on a daily basis in order to function effectively the next day at work, so the daughter would give her full support in this as well. The daughter did everything she could at her age to get things working at home. She knew that the father is incapable to support the family, so, she need to extend her full support in every possible way to the mother so that she can be a working lady. As said earlier, all this consumed the daughter completely.

The daughter is all consumed in and out but the father does not seem to realize this at all. That's why, as soon as she started earning (few weeks back), he is in the "extracting mode". He wants all, the same attitude which he has with the mother since the day she has been earning. Till now, she was being used by the mother. Now, it's father's turn. He thinks that since the daughter is good in studies and has backed a decent job, she will bring more and more money into the house. This money, will, in turn, be used to fulfill the family's wishes and earn him more and more respect. The father, poor selfish brat, is ready to consume the daughter one more time but this time, it is in a different way. Interesting! Earlier she was being consumed in the role of a "docile homemaker daughter", now she will be consumed in "independent breadwinner style". The irony of the situation is that both the roles have been written down by the father , the only difference is that this time the father is playing from frontfoot. The interesting thing to know will be that whether the daughter will manage to go with the flow or will she stop to change the course of her life by choosing healing over hurting?

CHAPTER FIFTEEN

It feels like a newborn. She wants to start all over again!

These 25 years of her life, the daughter has spent in stopping the domestic violence. Nothing else mattered. Every other thing was secondary. In fact, the secondary thing was also overcoming the domestic violence. Nothing else ever mattered. This is how it has been. Mind and heart was always occupied with the pain of the father's domestic violence. And now when the father shows "Jaa simran, jeele apni zindagi" kind of attitude to her for the very first time in her life, the daughter is simply spellbound. She does not know how to respond, she is neutral, as if she has entered into the world for the very first time, just like a new born.

Why newborn?? Because when all through her life she has felt only one kind of emotion, she does not know how to respond to other emotions. Just like a newborn, she does not know that what is her take on life. Just like a newborn, she does not know that what are her beliefs, what is her love, what is that one thing she is passionate about, what is one thing she hates doing. The credit to all this goes to the father mainly. Throughout these years, he had made the house into such a prominent warzone where only one thing happened : chaos, chaos and chaos.

The father never gave a chance to the daughter to feel any emotion other than pain, pain generated due to sheer domestic violence. When she used to go to school, the morning used to be filled with the aggressive abuses and shouts of the father. The same thing used to go in her mind during the school hours. As soon as she used to come back from school, the same tape recorder of the father used to be on again. Whatever may be the reason, be it the frustration on the mother or the fact that the kitchen is undone or the fact that the house is not properly clean or the fact that the things are not at its place in the house, everything used to be primarily directed towards the daughter. Since the mother, being working, never used to be available all the time to listen, so the father used to enjoy the liberty to throw mother's share of agonies also on the daughter. Whatever complaints he used to have from the mother would also come into the daughter's share because she was busy working. And daughter was free!! Free to be tortured!! All this was more than enough to occupy all the space in the daughter's brain and heart. So, she never got the opportunity to give importance to anything else.

Presently, she has just started earning money and for the father, the life of his victims (the mother and the daughter) is divided into two parts: one is before they are earning and the second is after they start earning. As soon as the second part of your life starts, the father gives you every liberty on this earth. The only thing that he wants in return is that you perform all his financial duties. In the daughter's case, that duty would be to fund the younger sister's education. And now for a person who has surrendered all her life to the wishes of the father so that domestic violence can be avoided, how can you expect her to be the controlling one?? In the first part, the father wanted to be the daughter to be the submissive one. In the second part, he wants sher to be the controlling one. How is this possible??

For the daughter, life has always worked at the mercy of the father. The father has always moulded her the way he wanted. He played tactics to make her the mother's best replacement at home so that the house duties do not fall upon him. She became so. He played tactics to make her self-sufficient at such an early age that she takes care of herself in the best possible way thus decreasing the burden on him or on the mother. She became so. She did her studies responsibly and never gave them the chance to worry about the same. Moreover, she did whatever was required to keep the situation calm at home. Whatever she does, she keeps the father in mind. It is not out of respect but out of fear, so that domestic violence does not happen. But the moment she has started earning, she is seeing different side of the father. A side which has let go of every small thing which used to be the biggest reason of scolding in the daughter's life, and sometimes even of beatings. He now justifies everything with the fact that since the daughter is earning, anything and everything is fine. All this feels so strange to the daughter that she does not know how to respond. This new second part attitude of the father seems so unusual to her that she is not able to make peace with it till date. In fact, whatever little respect she had left for the father is also now lost once she has seen his new behavior towards her.

Every memory dented with the pain of domestic violence. Every occasion smeared in the chaos of domestic violence. When she looks back, this is what she gets. That's why, she wants to start all over again. She wants to live her life again!! She wants to relive each and every moment and make up for the lost time. This time, when she goes back, there would be no domestic violence, every memory would be as uninterrupted with the pain of domestic violence as possible. She would enjoy every moment, form opinion over things and have a personality of her own, a personality which would know that what are its likes and dislikes, what are its beliefs!! A personality which would care to be itself is what she will form. A personality unburdened with the brutality of any kind of domestic violence is what she will form. She would feel things as they are and there will be nothing brutal like domestic violence to take over her likings. She would be independent in the truest sense possible. This independence is what she is looking for, not the one which the father guarantees to give her through his brutal rules of life which states only one thing to the ladies of the house : At any cost, start earning and I (the father) will set you free. Give him the money and he will rejoice and yet, he will hurt you!!

Everybody wants a second chance in their lives. This way everybody would ask for a second chance from god. What is so special in the case of the daughter? What is so different in this story?? The special thing here is the desire to be free the way she wants to be. The daughter does not want a second chance to be achieve a higher professional goal or to make her parents more proud through her achievements. She wants a second chance to feel things in the right way, as they are meant to be. Her first life did not allow her the liberty to feel any moment because everything was very intensely coated with the pain of domestic violence. There are possibilities that after 25 years, she would land up into the same job, doing the same work as she is doing today but this is no the point. The point is that she will be free the way she wanted to be. She will be free from the shackles of domestic violence which has been an integral part of her life for the last 25 years, it has perhaps been the only thing in her life for the last 25 years, overshadowing each and every other thing of her life. It is high time that she is freed from this chaos. And you know what? In her second life, when she reaches the present day, there would be no dual thinking going on in her mind that whether it is okay to be a working lady or not?? She would be free from this perplexed situation and this would be the greatest accomplishment of her life.

CHAPTER SIXTEEN

She does not want to fight anymore. It kills her.

She has started earning money, just like her mother. Her perplexity is still on. Inspite of this, she goes on. Her mother used to and still fights for her rights with the father. She used to and still defends her point endlessly to the father, creating more and more violent atmosphere in the house. But the daughter does not. She does not want the history to repeat because there is a younger one living in the house. What to talk about the younger one, her own self does not hold even 0.00000000001 percent ability to fight back. All gone in saving the mother.

She believes that the biggest mistake which the mother did in her life is that she gave the key to her heart and mind to the father, by responding to each and every fight which the father used to initiate. She does not want to do this. She is anyway in a perplexed state, a state from where everything feels right and wrong at the same time. She is in no craze to be financially independent and in no mood to prove her might (intellectually, ethically or physically) to the father. All she wants is peace to prevail because she has nothing to lose and no desires at this point.

No matter how hard the father tries to provoke her to fight back and respond, she does not. At least this is what she was suppose to learn from the mistakes of the mother. But she does not blame the mother for the behavioural mistake of fighting endlessly because the mother did not have any other option. She had to go solo, take every decision by herself and defend it in order to move forward. The daughter has the option to change the course of the story by being neutral and detached. The mother did not have, she had to earn, she had to earn for the family, she had to be happy, she had to be happy for the family.

The daughter wants to stay still and reconcile, reconcile with the present situation. But she cannot. This is the most unfortunate thing in her life right now. She cannot reconcile with the present circumstances. The moment which she feared all her life has come now. It is right in front of her eyes. She cannot reconcile with the fact that the father is behaving and will continue to behave in the exact same brutal way in which he behaves with her working mother. He is so afraid that the ladies might give up their jobs and stop earning if they face difficulties in their professional lives that he constantly keeps them in terror. This way, he keeps the offices to be a better place than the house, in the minds of the ladies. He wants everybody to be working and earning money, except himself !! The daughter cannot reconcile with the fact that he will make her go through the same toxic growth process which the mother went through. She cannot reconcile with the fact that the younger sister will go through the same pain and suffering which she went through all these years by defending the mother. She is afraid that now the father will be as cruel and demanding with the younger sister as he was with her when she was not earning. Everything that happened with her when she was at home and mother was outside working, all that will happen with the younger sister. All the howling, shouting, beating and abusing will now be directed towards the younger sister. And the most heart-wrecking and fearsome fact is that all this is coming true!! All this has already started happening.

She cannot move forward, she cannot stay still, she cannot go back in time. In every way, she is screwed. This is how 25 years of domestic violence hits you!! It takes away all your energy, your zeal and yet you need to move forward in life.

CHAPTER SEVENTEEN

Ripped and wrecked, more than ever

The father has ripped the daughter of self-respect, anger, pride, humanity, peace, sense of justice and yet he wants more! The never ending fight with the daughter and the mother has made the daughter lose so much that she has always turned up to be ripped and wrecked. This is how she has spent her entire life till now : ripped and wrecked. But see the irony of the situation. The father wants more!! Someone who has spent her entire life giving away everything she had so that peace can prevail in the house, how can she possibly give more??

As mentioned earlier, living ripped and wrecked is nothing new for the daughter. She has learnt to live this way. But something which is disastrously wrong this time is the fact that the wrongdoings of the father and the mother is ripping her off of humanity which she has for them. This humanity which she has towards the couple has always managed to stand the test of time, irrespective of the fact that they have always kept their own issues as the main thing and managed to fight endlessly over them. This time the daughter is being ripped to an extent that she will be beyond repair.

In a place where domestic violence has been the utmost thing, the daughter has always understood the importance of little moments of happiness. So, she has always tired to do her bit. Moreover, domestic violence has taken so much space in the house that there is no space for growth. Gradually, the issues of the couple had made them as well as the house so full of themselves that the daughter literally did not exist. Her being there was just a formality. And she completely got this since day one! She got this big time! Therefore, whatever little instances of growth she got, she used them to the fullest and returned the favour to the couple through good results. She has always been grateful to the couple that that they gave her these growth moments because she did not even expect these! It is in these spurring growth moments that she managed to excel in her studies, her trainings and writing work. These three things served as her lifelines just to sail through her ripped and wrecked life. But the father did not get this!!! As soon as he got the chance, he decided to exploit these talents of the daughter in a pressurized and violent manner, thus making her ripped and wrecked more than ever. And he calls it empowerment, perhaps women empowerment. Such is the evil doing of the father.

Imagine a wall filled with deep veins of cracks running all over it. This wall is the daughter's life and these deep cracks symbolize the domestic violence tragedies, scars and pain in her life. Since years of domestic violence can do no good to anybody, it is very much obvious that the foundation of the wall is also utterly weak. Now the question here is that if the gardener hides the weakness of the wall by decorating its cracks using beautiful climber plants like grapevines, honeysuckles etc., should it be misunderstood that the wall is very strong and is very much capable to offer support to anyone who leans against it? No, certainly not. This is what the father needs to understand. Just because the daughter has managed to keep her life sane during all these years by indulging and doing well in every job she was given at hand, it doesn't mean that she has remained untouched by the viciousness of domestic violence going on in the house. The deadly environment of the house has affected her to the same extent as it has affected him or the mother. At times, even more because the couple even got the chance to take out the frustration on each other but the daughter never allowed this chance. The father was too strict to hear any of her painful feelings and the mother was too wrecked herself to take any more pain. So, all she did was try and live with it. Hence, the father has absolutely no right to even think of exploiting her more via her talents because she is ripped and wrecked more than ever.

CHAPTER EIGHTEEN

Those cold memories haunt her

Life has become very difficult for the daughter. She is going through the mental trauma of domestic violence twice. Once, when it all happened with the mother and second time, when it is all happening with her. Life could not be more difficult for her. From the day she has started earning and become a fully independent (in terms of the father) girl, she always lives in the fear that she will be treated in the same ruthless manner as her working mother is treated every second. Exactly the same is happening!! Things have started to take place in the same way which give her a picture that history will repeat. And there is nobody to stop. The daughter herself is in such a deep state of shock and fear that some external force is needed to keep things moving. She does not want to move ahead in life. The very basic feeling of moving ahead in life and experiencing it has gone. What a pity! Nothing can be more wrong.

Every single moment of violence repeats in her head. It cripples her. Everytime when the father used to blame the mother for being who she was, everytime when he used to blame her for getting in his way of professional progress and ruining it all for him : she remembers it all.

She remembers all the chaos which would happen in the house just because the working mother did not cook up dinner on time. Each and every act of domestic violence revolves in her head and eventually stops her to move forward. Can all this be more crippling for the daughter??

After seeing domestic violence in the house for the last 25 years, one thing is very clear to the daughter. Her life would have been way better if her mother was not earning!! For someone who wants to stand on his own feet and expects mental support but nothing else, the mother was not the right choice for the father. The mother had so much to offer than just the needed emotional support. And this is what ruined everybody's life. It may be so that the daughter is wrong. Maybe the father would have turned out to be the same ruthless animal which he is today. But there are so many instances which show that a non-earning mother would have been better in this case. One very clear instance which the daughter still remembers is when the father had taken up a well-earning new job as the factory manager. The very first night after returning from his first day of new job, he conveyed to the mother very clearly about his intentions of her taking care of the children while he will be the breadwinner. But the mother had to be the mother. She listened from one ear and let it go from the other. In short, the father's words of wisdom made no sense to her. The very next day she was out looking for a job and spending extra hours on it, leaving behind the family. It is that day and today that peace could never be restored in the family. From that day, the shift of power and popularity from the father to the mother was so evident that it consumed every ounce of peace existing in the daughter's life. Being in competition with your own husband is not bad but it should not be done at the expense of his career. It is not only bad for the wife but also for the children who are at no fault of their own.

A different level of domestic violence started in the family after the mother decided to work irrespective of the fact that the father asked her to be at home and look after the kids. This is because the father could not give his hundred percent to the job because of various reasons while the mother was doing exceptionally well with her new job. Things professionally got very well for the mother as she received various promotions and started earning well. On the other hand, the father was totally drowning professionally as he lost his job in a couple of months. Now who is at fault here?? The mother or the father? The daughter is clear. The answer is the father, because man is responsible for his own actions. Then why is she so angry with the mother?? Why is she not in favour of her mother being working?? This is because an earning mother has come at a cost of a suppressed daughter. All these years, the pain, anger and grief of professional downfalls as well as the increasing jealousy towards mother's growing progress has taken a toll on father's mental well-being. As a result, he chose to vent out his frustration on the daughter. In fact, he left no chance to belittle the daughter when the mother was not at home. The mental drift between the minds of the couple when one was touching skies and the other was falling on the ground has been very painful for the daughter. In order to survive these times, she had to witness endless ego fights happening between the couple, lots and lots of beatings and what not. She had witnessed it all. Everything was taking place just in front of her eyes. That's why when its her time to do professionally well, she does not even feel like moving towards it because the past cripples her. In no way, she wants to do well in life at the cost of the father's happiness. As the father is trying hard till date to grab a good job (because of his fluctuating career) and perform well at it, she does not want to come in the way at all. She does not have the ability to go through the same trauma all over again. Let the father have the chance to blame no one but himself for his shortcomings. The daughter does not want to be a part of this.

CHAPTER NINETEEN

The Great Repentance : break then make initiative

The father follows a pattern and the daughter knows it. She knows every block of the chessboard so discreetly that it might stun the father. How? The answer is simple, because he has played the game once with the mother. The daughter has witnessed everything so closely at that time she has become above all this. The father's game cards are all out.

Same game, same pattern, same tricks. What is new this time? " The Great Repentance", the only move of the father which will make all the difference this time. The daughter calls this great repentance of the father as "break then make" initiative. One must not take this move to be a simple one in any way. It involves years of plotting and planning (pun intended) of the father because this move has the capability to wash away all the sins which he committed towards his daughter thus giving her a new life. Now, wait a minute. Do you think that the father has been doing all this for the daughter?? Has he been planning this major move for the daughter's benefit?? No, not at all. He has been doing all this for only and only himself. He very well knows that what he has done to his daughter in the name of "wife empowerment" is absolutely wrong. As a result, he wants to get rid of the sins committed by giving the daughter a new identity. It is his great repentance towards the daughter. Everything could have gone ahead as planned by the father and he would have achieved nirvana in his own nonsense sense. But one small problem cropped up : the daughter. The saddest part of the father's planning and plotting is his inconsideration of the daughter. While planning the whole game and its strategies, he forgot to take into account the daughter. Since for the last twenty-five years she has been a silent supporter of the "family peace restoration group" (pun intended), he has forgotten her. He has forgotten that she is also a living being who can and will retaliate when the time is right for her.

Every bit of domestic violence in the house would be somehow related to the clashing of the couple's work domains. The father used to work and earn. The mother used to do the same. Nobody lived happily ever after. Why? Because many domains clashed which resulted into war but nothing else. Firstly, as wealth poured in, its management became a matter of discussion which could not be sorted by the couple. Secondly, as one of them lost the job, the other would automatically become increasingly dominant in all the decisions of the house. Slowly and gradually, the power would go into one person's hand. In this case, that one person was the mother. The father not at all liked this. Thirdly, when one starts earning, he/she wants to live life his/ her own way with a certain level of comfort. This is what the mother was doing. Again, the father did not like this because he could not bear the fact that a women in his house is living a life on his own terms. The daughter has seen all this for the last 25 years. So, all this has caused her to form one very firm belief. She strictly believes that out of two people married to each other, it is better if one takes care of the house and kids while the other one earns money. She obviously does not want everyone to follow it. It is for her own self as she wants to keep her life simple and sorted. Moreover, after facing domestic violence for such substantial amount of time, she has come to the conclusion that her married life would be very easy if there is no clashing of domains between the couple. Therefore, she is an avid supporter of one person earning and the other non-earning.

The father does not like this philosophy of the daughter. Why? Because he wants to see his daughter win every battle of life with flying colours, because he wants her to face every challenge of life and come out victorious, because he wants her to become self-sufficient in every manner. No, absolutely not!!! The pure and the only motive of the father is "the great repentance". It is his favourite new move which he is dying to play. It gives him a purpose to live. And the daughter's life purpose is to expose this purpose of his!!! She wants to show to the world that women empowerment can be wrapped with such evil intentions.

Why does the daughter call this repentance of the father towards her as "great"? Moreover, why does she denote it as "break then make initiative"? Actually, there are many reasons behind this but one thing is for sure that this "repentance move" of the father is the greatest in the history of planning and plotting (pun intended). It is a truly a mark of the father's evil thinking abilities. This repentance is the greatest of all because if implemented properly, it has the ability to give meaning to two lives (according to the father). One is of the father of course, because he will achieve his nirvana as he believes that his sins towards the daughter will be washed away if she becomes self-dependent through his help and thinking. Second life is that of the daughter, as she will establish a new identity of her own by earning and making a name for herself. This will in turn help her to forget the trauma of domestic violence which is now deeply embedded in her heart and mind.

It is a "break then make" initiative because this is what the father does. He will first fully break the daughter of her present belief system that one person earning is fine. He will do so by sending her to any and every work thus making her to earn money. This way the daughter will eventually become hopeless and surrender to him. Once things will start going according to him, he will make the daughter earn more and more money through job changes and promotions. This is his game plan. Now the biggest question is: What will the daughter do amidst all this? Will she succumb to the challenges thrown at her by the father or will she make her own path in her own way?? Let's see how it all goes for her.

CHAPTER TWENTY

Welcome to the " Third Generation"

If earning for a living is to be considered as a sign of utmost empowerment, the daughter would like to divide the generations of people into three categories. In the first generation, men earned and felt empowered. In the second generation, both men and women earned and felt empowered. In the third generation?? What the third generation does will be very well defined by the fact that how sustainable was the empowerment story of the second generation!!! It will now all depend on how mutually nourishing this empowerment was when both men and women were given an equal opportunity to grow!!! God forbid, if this concept of equal opportunity has been more tarnishing instead of being more productive, then this is where lies an opportunity for the third generation to outgrow and outshine the second generation. The day when both men and women enjoy empowerment in the truest sense in the same house at the same time, that is when third generation will derive true meaning of their own existence.

The daughter is witnessing this transformation from first generation to the third in front of her own eyes in her own very house! In fact, the way things have been turning into just next level with time has made her to use the term "generation". This word "generation" used in the chapter marks the huge shift she has witnessed in the house as the family went from a zone of "man empowerment" to "women empowerment" and then to the present zone wherein the daughter has to decide the future course of action. Why is it being called a "women empowerment" zone and not "both men and women empowerment" zone?? Why the second generation in the daughter's house being denoted as "women empowerment" and not "both men and women empowerment"?? Because this is what the daughter has seen!! This is what the daughter has witnessed for her entire life : Women, her mother being empowered by her father at the cost of his own happiness. Ultimately, the father is repenting because of this as the foundation of coexistence is being broken between the couple. All this has actually culminated into domestic violence which knows no end!! Furthermore, what is this present zone?? Which is this zone in which the daughter is right now?? It is the zone of dilemma!!! The zone of sheer, utter, constant dilemma. It is the zone of third generation wherein she knows what is the right thing to do but has no clue how to do it. She is very well aware that her generation has to be about a society, in fact about homes wherein both empowered man and women can peacefully coexist but how can she achieve this? How can she achieve this for her own house and set an example for the world?

The daughter fails to understand that which path is she suppose to follow?? What is the truth?? The father who never earned much himself but wants everybody around him to be financially empowered? Or the mother who has managed to be empowered to in each and every bloody way at the cost of her own huband and kids? Who is right? Why is this all so complicated for her? Which path is she suppose to tread on?

CHAPTER TWENTY-ONE

Kill her or heal her

At this point of her life, the daughter demands a healing. She demands a healing touch from the universe, from her parents, from anywhere......she needs it, she needs it badly. As a person needs to breathe to keep living, she wants healing for her survival. Even more than breathing!!! For some people, healing must be a momentary affair wherein they can survive even if it is not there. But for the daughter, it is now her right. She feels that it is that point in her life where she has lost everything and yet her parents ask more from her. From where is she suppose to give them more if she herself is not feeling alright?

If the father has divided the whole life of his daughter into two categories wherein the first one he feels that it is he who did everything and in the second the daughter has to return the favour, then he is wrong. This bifurcation of his is wrong. It is his absolute misconception that by the time the daughter was not financially independent, it is he who did all the sacrifices. What he did was not sacrifice, what he did was sheer violence. A domestic violence which has no justification. If there is anybody who actually sacrificed is the mother and the daughter who faced each and every situation bravely rather than succumbing to the violence in the house. They still do. What the father did was hiding from his problems and being so dominant in the house so that nobody can even think of blaming him for his failures in life. All one was suppose to do was to fight for his survival in the house so that one can get a bed to sleep and three times meal to live. This is how things have been in the house. This may seem to be the story of every other household where the father is strict and domestic violence happens. But it is not. Why not? How is this story different?? It is different because it is not discussing about the turmoil of the generation who actually fought, quarreled, cut each other's throat to prove themselves right. It is actually concerned about the next generation who is left with so much negativity and yet they are asked to function normally like any other human being. Is that even possible? Is that even a question for the father to ask to the daughter that what all she can offer to him in terms of happiness, finance, goodwill, pride etc once she becomes an adult ? In fact, this generation need all this! This is how much they have been broken by the domestic violence. It shakes their confidence. It shakes their very existence on this planet. They start doubting everything around them. This becomes worse when both the parents of conflicting views and ideologies start to impose their thinking on the child. The child becomes confused and surrenders to the circumstance. This is what is happening with the daughter. She is right now confused in every aspect of her life. Eventually, this confusion has paved way for grief, anger, anxiety, pain in her life because the parents' expectations are rising and she is still adapting to the ever changing hostile environment in the house.

Twenty-five years of her stay in the house has made her very clear that she can achieve nothing more than the basic survival in the house. As a result, her expectations from herself as well as the family has been very minimal. Everything other than the sleep and food has been a bonus for her. But as the tension between the couple in the house keeps on growing, it is even difficult to breathe in the house. What to talk about being empowered, which the father apparently wants everybody to be! This is what is his life motto. It feels really very good to hear such stuff from the father and one may feel really motivated but when it comes to actually giving conditions to achieve the same, it is next to impossible. The house and its members (except the father) get too used up in bearing the brunt of one empowered lady, they will become too wrecked if there will be two in the house. Why? Empowerment is good, what is there to "bear"? In the daughter's house, empowerment is much about bearing rather than enjoying. This is because in her house, empowerment means that you need to bring money in the house and nothing more. The father wants money. This is empowerment. The mother succumbed to this. The daughter does not. She does not even want to earn for herself in an environment which is based on such cheap and filthy ideology. She has named this ideology of the father as "half empowered-half impaired" as this is what he has made the mother. The mother eats, sleeps, earns, everything she does, even her breathing, everything happens at the father's consent. The remote control of her life is with him. The sad part is that somewhere deep down in her heart, she knows this thing but denies it even to herself. Women empowerment can be done with such evil intentions where you feel that is it really empowerment of any sort!!! The daughter does not want to support this at all, that's why from the moment she has started earning, she does not enjoy it all. She has seen that ugly side of women empowerment which has made her life very bitter and tough. She needs healing.

The daughter expects healing. Is she wrong in this expectation of hers or is she right? Can it really happen? Time only has the answer for this. Who or what will heal the daughter? There is a very inspiring quote by actress Sushmita Sen which says "The only way to go beyond things is to go through them". If the daughter is determined to heal herself, she needs to face every challenge of her life. Instead of escaping, she needs to be there no matter how hard the situation is. If she wants to go beyond her trauma of domestic violence and ugly empowerment, she has to go through the situation. As said earlier, it is all very hard for the daughter because she feels that she is going through every bit of violence twice (one when it all happened with her mother and now she herself) but she needs to overcome it. How can she overcome it? By being positive and keep moving forward in her life. She has to be her own healer. Happiness, healing...everything comes from within. The only thing matters is your determination. No matter how angry she might be at her life right now, she is very well aware of this ultimate truth. Let's see how well she will be able to implement this in her life.

CHAPTER TWENTY-TWO

Women Empowerment : It's time we do it right!

Who is an empowered women? A women who chooses to be a simple housewife or a women who chooses to be a working lady? A women who enjoys wearing a cool jacket and a shiny miniskirt or a women who always prefers wearing an ethnic wear? A women who earns her living by taking evening dance classes or a women who earns her living by being a college professor? Who decides the criteria of being an "empowered women"? The women herself. Nobody else has the right to define it. This is what the daughter wants the father to understand.

Everytime the father sets a definition of an "empowered women" in front of the daughter, she wants to say it loud and clear that he cannot set her limits. She has been wanting to say this since the last 25 years but everytime he molds the definition as per his own convenience. A convenience which would encourage money flow into the household, this is his ultimate motto. Nothing else matters to him. What if the daughter wants to simply enjoy being a housewife, a homemaker? She is not allowed to do that.

The reason is her father. She completely gets the point that in order to sustain ourselves, we all need to earn money but why does the father always link this aspect with the ultimate definition of "women empowerment"? It is here that the cunningness of the father reflects to the daughter as crystal clear and she denies earning.

This is what the father had been doing the mother for the last 25 years and the daughter is tired of watching this. She wants to break this cycle because this cycle has only lead to more and more domestic violence which now knows no boundaries. This is how the father wraps his evil intentions in the name of "women empowerment". For the last 25 years, the women of the house have been taught the lesson of "women empowerment" by the father and when they actually start blossoming the way they want to, their wings are torn off and sticked back the way he wants it to be!!! This is the harsh reality. An empowered women who is empowered by the father, of the father and with the father. Nothing else is acceptable to him. This all is completely unacceptable to the daughter as she doesn't call this process being followed in the house as "empowerment", she calls it "butchering" wherein a person is deprived of their self-respect, their pride, their self-worth. Literally, everything is taken away from the person, what is left is a puppet who surrenders in front of the "highest revered figure of the house" (pun intended), the father.

The daughter very strictly feels that the mother is nothing without the father. This is how empowered she is. It may sound very " traditionally romantic" for now but the people who have to live with such kind of couple have to pay a heavy price. The two daughters. The mother would have been empowered in the real sense when she could live the way she wants to, when she could breathe in free air but all this is nowhere happening. Right now, she is a pawn of the father and with she being the pawn, the two daughters are left with no choice than to be another two pawns. The daughter feels that this needs to stop and even if it means sacrificing her career, she will do it! She does not and cannot live this way. She refuses to live in a house which is a part of a democratic country but still not democratic. She refuses to be a part of a house where one person gets to decide the fate of the other three and functions as the ultimate god. If the father really wants to be a god, he should have allowed his ladies to make mistakes and learn and become strong in the process, rather than regulating every part of their life and plan it in such a way that they would ultimately surrender to him. What a brilliant masterstroke from the father's side! But his biggest defeat is that the daughter has understood his game plan and is determined to stop this, by hook or by crook.

For almost her entire life she has summoned to the dictatorship of the father because of fear of domestic violence and now when she has become old enough to decide her own fate, she wants to prove through her actions that " she is not his pawn". She wants to prove him that she has the ability to decide her own fate in her own desired way. Also, she wants to relieve him of his job of "empowering the women of the house" which he has taken up without their consent. The mother would be fine with this trend as she enjoys earning and spending the money the way she wants to but the daughters clearly don't appreciate this at all. They want to define their own goals and even if they fail in achieving these goals, they won't mind because they know that it is the part of the process. Most importantly, they also know that the way their mother has been empowered by the father is not the real empowerment. Real empowerment comes from taking up new challenges in life, putting yourself into the risk of the unknown and then testing your willpower. All this must come from within, not from the father's ultimate fear of domestic violence or the fear of making money. Real empowerment makes you an independent person in every way and not just financially.

CHAPTER TWENTY-THREE

This time the daughter wants to be a complete failure!

The daughter is tired of listening this from the father that the mother has stopped her career growth, the mother has shadowed her. She wants to give him the fullest chance. She wants to do nothing and just be a mere spectator. She wants to put herself at halt, a big pause, wherein she would only be doing the basic: breathing, eating food, bathing, going to washroom for nature's call. She just wants to exist and do nothing else. Such is the fear of the domestic violence in her head and heart. Her question is : When all the fuss is about blaming the mother that her empowerment has stopped him to progress and led him to depression, then why not give the father a chance to make up for the loss? Why not give him a free ground to play as he wants? Why not give him all the spotlight to perform if he is so brilliant (pun intended)? The father, who has become so godly brilliant that he has been empowering the ladies of the house since decades, why not give him a chance to be empowered? Let the maker be the player play in full swing for once and let us see if he has the ability to actually perform instead of giving just big vague lectures on "women empowerment". Is this whole drama of "women empowerment" is just an excuse to hide his own incompetence of earning money for the family or does he really has the passion to earn for the family if given a purely fair chance?

The daughter feels that the father has the passion needed for being "financially independent" (one particular which he wants everybody to be) and be a star performer of the house but that passion comes in bouts. Since he has empowered the mother to an extent that everyone and everything is inevitably controlled by her, one can witness his bout of passion only in extreme adverse conditions (like extreme financial crisis or extreme need to prove his self-worth). So, the daughter wants his passion to flow at all times thus making him financially sufficient, a thing which he has long been trying to do by himself (pun intended).

The man who tells a women her real place by mistreating her wants her to see empowered. Why? This is something the daughter fails to understand. What is there that she is missing in the story? Hmm....... Is it the greed for money? Is it the need for praise that one would get by empowering her lady? What is this dual nature all about? What all is hidden behind this dual nature of the father? The daughter wants to know. She wants to actually find out that what is the most important intention of the father behind being such dual natured? Whatever it may be, she know it one hundred percent that it is not " empowering women". If it would all have been about "empowering women", he would not have suppressed the voice of the daughter to make his wife extra loud!!! This is not about women empowerment.

The father has insecurities which he is trying to fight through his daughter. At present, he has reached a point where he is done trying to outperform the mother careerwise and everything has gone in vain. The mother still outshines him. He has tried everything : anger, love, respect, violence. Although his bouts of passion have helped him to be earn the tag of "employed" many a times but he has never been able to sustain at any job for too long. So, what is his ultimate plan? The daughter! As everybody is a pawn for him, he is now using her to be in direct competition with the mother. Something which he has been trying to do since so long, he wants the daughter to do that. How can the daughter be so sure of this? Well, because she has instances to prove this! There have been times when the father has tried to behave as the "wicked" one and pump her for no reason so that she fights with the mother, the women who has taken care of her always and still does. Why would she fight with the mother? Just because she wants to save her career. No, she would not. This is where she is different from the father. No matter what, she will not fight with the mother if it is only for the sake of her career because her thirst for money and fame is still not that big as that of the father!

If space is what is needed by the father to grow and flourish as a fully independent man who earns well and lives life according to his own wish, the daughter wants to give her that space! She knows that she is giving her this space only to find out that he has been trying to hide his own insecurities behind the mother and now the daughter in the name of "women empowerment" but she still wants to! Why? Because she does not feel that it is the right time for her to flourish, chase her career and earn. She feels that while she was growing up she chose her mother (

because she was correct) and in the process of doing so, she has somehow suppressed her father. She has somehow hampered the father's progress. So, she feels that now its her turn to support him by giving him a free ground where he can play all by himself to win. Sometimes, all one needs is a fair chance. Although there is no doubt that he has always tried to perform whenever he has got chance and that is how his little bouts of passion became evident to the daughter but this time it would be very different. Because this time, he has a lot of experience, his desire to perform has grown to next level and now with age, he knows that he has not much chances left. Most importantly, this time he has got a very uninterested competitor who is willing to lose if he is ready to win !

CHAPTER TWENTY-FOUR

You cannot have best of both the worlds. Never!

A wife who walks every step according to his husband's will and at the same time, has her own voice!!! This does not happen. The father is asking for too much. In fact, he is asking for the unachievable. The daughter wants to tell this to him very eagerly, very desperately, very clearly, very loudly....... she wants to shout it out in his ears. She feels that the whole battle in his life has been about achieving this impossible balance which has consumed her life as well. She feels that the father should have decided it long time ago that what does he want from his wife.... is it the homemaker version or is it the empowered version?

She wants to applaud the father that he has tried to achieve the impossible through his wife but at the same time, she wants all her days back where she has witnessed unlimited chaos in the house because of all this!!! She wants a justification, she wants an apology from the father. She wants to hear from him that what he has done to her is wrong, very very wrong. In the quest of achieving the unachievable, he is accountable of destroying his life and he must repay it. Repay it at all cost!!! How can he repay it? The daughter wants that it is now high time that he must understand that an empowered soul has a mind of his own. He thinks, he speaks, he believes.....just the usual normal things which an empowered soul is supposed to do (pun intended) and he cannot and must not stop it!!! It is called blossoming into one's own personality and he must not mould it as per his own convenience. The mother has survived this battle with the father because she had daughter by her side and also, with all the money pouring in, she chose to live on her own terms by buying and shopping anytime in order to cheer up her mood. But how is the daughter suppose to bear all this and make her way? How can she possibly do it when she does not have the liberty to be her own self? Till now, she has been living with the belief that she needs to function according to her father's beliefs. The father's belief has been her own!!! She has no choice. She always did what she was suppose to do but now she denies. She denies it because her heart does not allow it. She does not want to be butchered by the father as the mother has been. She first wants the father to understand the real meaning of women empowerment and then she can live according to his plan. A man who does not know the real meaning of women empowerment and changes it according to his own convenience cannot be a mentor to the daughter.

Till now, the mother has been the empowered lady of the house who speaks her mind and the daughter has been the docile submissive lady of the house walking each and every step according to the father's will. In fact, supporting the mother by being her closest confidante has been the part of the father's plan which the daughter had to follow blindly!!! Truly, the father has achieved the unachievable (pun intended). But it's done now. The daughter cannot go on further like this. She needs a closure. Why? Why does she not live like the mother? Why does she also not earn and live according to her own wish by shopping, giggling, bossing around in the house? She cannot, even if she wants to. She cannot because she does not have the energy and time to fight endlessly with the father as the mother does, just because she has a mind of her own. She has fought enough to protect the mother and does not have the energy to fight all over again the same set of battles just because the father still doesn't understand the real meaning of empowered women.

Confused mind can be a boon for some but for many, a stable mind is the best thing. Moreover, you cannot have it all in life. You must choose. The daughter wants the father to understand this. He must take a stand, he must decide what he wants from his life, what he wants from his wife, what he wants from his daughter. These three decisions, the ones which differentiate the successful ones from the unsuccessful ones, must be taken by the father because it is already too late. He must not change as per his own convenience. The daughter wants to be kind enough to him by following him as soon as he takes three decisions but before that, she cannot be his follower. Every soul has its own charm and instead of butchering anybody's soul to make him function his way, he must direct his energy to fight his own fears. The daughter understands that with his wife being the empowered one in the house, there is not much room left for him to grown in the most usual way (the usual 9-5 job and monthly salary coming in) because this is how the clashes come in between the couple when the domains become common. Furthermore, as he has been fighting this same nonsense battle for the last

25 years with the mother, she also understands that he must be very very tired now. The daughter feels that the answer to his quest lies for now in "the change of domain", a zone which does not clash with the mother's personal and work space. Since she has been observing this for the last 25 years of her life that the father has been fighting for "space" in the house, be it careerwise, fame wise, respect wise, room wise and his way of thinking is such that he feels that all his problems can be answered if he becomes financially independent, the daughter feels that he must choose the path yet "unexplored" by the mother. The road less travelled is the only answer to his dilemma. Also, the daughter neither has the permission nor the courage to change his set of mind about linking financial independence to ultimate independence, she must go his way and help him achieve what he has truly wanted. What does the daughter mean by "the change of domain" and how is it going to benefit the father? So, basically he needs to work on things which is yet not done by the mother because those areas free from any kind of interference from the mother thus providing him the needed "space" to explore himself and be financially rewarding. He must write, write mathematics book which he has always wanted to do. He must sing songs (although he does sometimes and put it on the family watsapp group) but now, he must do it more often. In fact, he must start a youtube channel of the same.

Earlier, the daughter used to look at the father as a dictator who needs to be followed at all cost. As the mother started becoming financially independent and began sharing his responsibilities in this sector, she started getting little leeway from the father's dictatorship. As far as the youngest one in the house is concerned, she has always enjoyed father's love because he has a rule (which he tells very proudly) that the youngest child in the family is always loved by the father. Now, who is left? Who is left on whom he can vent out his anger? The daughter. Moroever, as she used to always stand by the mother to protect her from domestic violence in the house, she became the ultimate enemy of the father. She still is !!! Due to the hatred of the father towards her, she was so busy coping it and if possible, escaping it that she never got a chance to truly understand him. During this entire time, she never got a chance (in fact, she was not allowed by the father) to keep herself at his place and find out the real reason of his annoyance. She was never allowed to use her mind and still is not allowed but now she feels that it is high time to use it! Now, when she is standing on her own feet financially and the father has given her the permission to live her own way (because he loves money and gives ultimate freedom to anybody and everybody who brings money in the house), she now realizes what the father actually wants!!! What an irony! It took 25 years for her to look this aspect of life, where the father is alone, struggling and trying to win.

How come now? What is so different today? The difference if of the "urge to become empowered" within the daughter. Earlier, as the daughter used to abide by the father's each and every instruction, there was no chaos as the ultimate empowerment was achieved by the mother. Although the father used to try to seek his own share of empowerment in the house through his job but he could not sustain it for too long. So, the father used to feel the pain of feeling suppressed and crushed by the mother but the daughter was always indifferent to it. And why will she not be? She was bearing the pain of frustration borne by the father because of the mother. But now, the daughter is at the father's place. Or it can be said that she has been put at such a place by the father where her domains are clashing with the mother. Thus, the hidden dimension of the story is unleashing. The father must view the financial independence of the daughter as a chance to bring more money into the house but she views it as an opportunity to show father the way to establish himself in front of mother, a thing which he has always wanted to do. And for doing so, she really feels that he must start by understanding the real meaning of "women empowerment" and direct all his energy towards exploring the areas of work where the mother has not intruded yet, instead of butchering another women of the house (the daughter, first one being the mother) to suit his own comfort and temperament.

9 798886 298062

Printed by Libri Plureos GmbH in Hamburg, Germany